GOLF INSTRUCTOR'S LIBRARY

FROM THE FAIRWAY

GOLF INSTRUCTOR'S LIBRARY

FROM THE FAIRWAY

M I C H A E L   H O B B S

THE
APPLE
PRESS

A QUINTET BOOK

Published by The Apple Press
6 Blundell Street
London N7 9BH

ISBN 1-85076-280-5

This book was designed and produced by
Quintet Publishing Limited
6 Blundell Street
London N7 9BH

Creative Director: Terry Jeavons
Designer: Stuart Walden
Project Editors: David Barraclough, Lindsay Porter
Illustrator: Rob Shone
Photographer: Michael Hobbs

Typeset in Great Britain by
Central Southern Typesetters, Eastbourne
Manufactured in Hong Kong by
Regent Publishing Services Limited
Printed in Hong Kong by
Leefung-Asco Printers Limited

CONTENTS

PREFACE

I am a left-handed golfer. However, over the years I haven't found it difficult to follow golf instruction writing, which is traditionally directed at right-handers.

As a golf writer, I know that always mentioning each form of the golfing species is easily possible, but leads to many repetitive phrases that impair the readability of the book. As a left-hander I know we have learned to cope in a 90 per cent right-handed world. A right-hander, on the other hand, is far less able. I don't think he could follow a text written for left-handers – imagine him trying to use left-handed scissors or knock in a tack, grasping the hammer left-handed. What injuries and incompetence would result for this less adaptable and accomplished sector of the human species!

ACKNOWLEDGEMENTS

Above all, I should like to thank Grenville Warne for being a splendid model for my instructional photography. He gave up many hours throughout a whole season when he would surely far rather have been playing than demonstrating. His help has been invaluable.

I should like to thank my main golf club, Tracy Park near Bristol, England, for allowing me to carry out most of the instruction photography on its splendid 27 holes. I also thank other clubs for more limited photographic facilities.

The club's professional, Grant Aitken, and his son and assistant professional Kelvin, have also been invariably helpful with advice, information and allowing me to use equipment for illustrations.

At Quintet Publishing, I should particularly like to thank David Barraclough for his continuous work throughout the project and also Peter Arnold who was responsible for the detailed copy editing. My thanks are also due to Rob Shone for his production of drawings and diagrams and the design team at Bridgewater Design.

Michael Hobbs   Worcester, England

INTRODUCTION

The fairway, in golf, is defined as any closely-mown area 'through the green'. That is, any part of the golf course to which you are expected to hit the ball, except tees and greens.

This means a great variety of shots, using every club in the bag – including driver and putter. Length can be anything from a shot of anything up to 300 yards with a driver from a good lie, to a putt from the fringe of a green to a flag just a few yards away.

Playing from the fairway with woods and irons is equally broad in scope as far as swing speeds are concerned, and can achieve anything from a full shot to the most delicate pitch and chip.

LEFT: Playing from the fairway – the closely-mown area between tee and green – demands shots as varied as a full-blooded wood, a sweetly struck mid-iron and a delicate chip a few yards out from the flag.

7

THE FAIRWAY WOODS

This term is really one of the silliest in golf. Other materials have partly replaced wood – predominantely metal – but to date, no one has invented a better term. At least, everyone knows what it means.

THE DRIVER

Yes – your driver really is a fairway wood, but how many golfers ever dream of using it except from a tee peg?

To some extent, there is wisdom in this attitude. Certainly, the driver is mostly to be used when the ball is perched up invitingly and because it is the longest club in the set, it should, in theory, be the most difficult one to use consistently. However, there are certain situations when the driver is well worth considering

WHEN YOUR BALL IS LYING VERY WELL
In this case, the grassy lie acts as a kind of substitute for a tee peg. On some courses – certain links for example, where the fine grasses tend to grow sideways rather than upwards – you will seldom find such a lie. On others, where growth is dense, or where the strain of grass seems to support the ball, very good lies are by no means rare.

When you find one such lie, and you also need distance, the driver could be the club to use. Basically, the shot is approached in just the same way as a normal tee shot, with just one or two slight differences.

If you are an 'animal' on the tee, always striving for the big hit and not worrying too much about accuracy, then you will have to make adjustments. Your ball may be sitting up and begging for it, but it's still much easier to duff your shot than it is from a tee peg.

Just for once, subdue your animal instincts, and swing at about 80 per cent power. You can help to control the

LEFT AND BELOW: Most golfers would only think of using their driver from the tee. However, provided you have a good lie, grip the club a couple of inches lower than usual and swing smoothly at less than full power, there is nothing to stop you playing this club from the fairway. On the other hand you can use an iron from the tee.

clubhead by sacrificing a little distance and gripping the club a couple of inches lower down.

WHEN YOU NEED TO KEEP THE BALL LOW

This can be the case in either of two situations: when an obstacle, often low branches, lies ahead of you, and when you need to keep your ball down, under the main force of a wind.

Even if your ball isn't lying ideally, you should be prepared to use your driver in these circumstances. Your club loft is unlikely to be more than 12 degrees, so the same swing as you would use with a 3 wood is mechanically certain to propel your ball along a lower trajectory.

There is, of course, a danger of half-thinning the ball if your lie is unfavourable, but even this can be an advantage: your ball is even more certain to keep low, and although it won't fly a long way, ought to get plenty of run in average or dry conditions.

IF YOU HABITUALLY SLICE OR FADE

If you're one of these players, you won't have much difficulty in getting your ball airborne, whatever the loft of the club you're using . But you will find the extra length that your driver will give you from the fairway very useful. You know – the club isn't really as difficult as all that.

Conversely, if you hook or draw the ball, you'd probably do best to leave the driver alone, unless, that is, you are a good enough striker to feel full of confidence. The driver is always worth considering, however, if a low, running shot seems to be what the situation demands.

IF YOU HIT DOWN WITH ALL YOUR WOODS

A driver shot from a tee peg is normally played with the clubhead travelling on the level at impact, or even slightly on the upswing. Many players, however, hit down on the ball – which isn't necessarily the mark of an inferior player.

Early in his professional career, Arnold Palmer didn't just hit down on the ball – he deliberately aimed to hit the ground first and the ball second. His club bounced into the ball, especially on hard ground.

Hitting down on the ball with a driver does reduce the length obtained from the tee. The ball is hit a slightly glancing blow, and not with a flow along the target line. There is also more backspin. The usual result is more height and less carry and run.

However, this can be turned to advantage when playing from the fairway. Such a player might be every bit as long as he would be from a tee peg.

BELOW: When the ball is teed-up it is fairly easy to get it airborne with a driver. Although it is harder to do this from the fairway, hitting down into the back of the ball will impart more backspin and help to give you more height.

OPPOSITE: For greater accuracy without loss of distance, many professionals carry a 1-iron in place of a 4-wood.

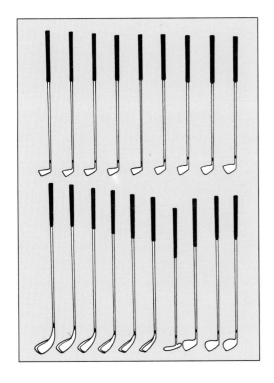

ABOVE: A full range of clubs from which a player can choose to make up a full set of 14. Top row – irons (1-9); Bottom row – woods (driver, 2, 3, 4 and 7), a putter, two wedges and a sand wedge.

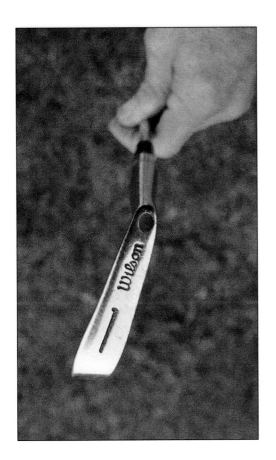

I remember talking to Dai Rees, the great Welsh golfer, some years ago, on the subject of Henry Cotton and his length. He told me that the great triple Open Champion wasn't exceptionally long from the tee, but that he was when using his driver from the fairway.

At his best, Cotton was one of the few great players who tried to hit every shot straight (Byron Nelson is the only other example I can think of), so he didn't have the advantages which a fader does, for example. However, in his very great days, Cotton was a striker of superb precision: perhaps he didn't have to restrict his swing to maintain control when using his driver from the fairway.

■ IF YOUR DRIVER HAS MORE LOFT THAN THE AVERAGE -

There are no rules laid down for the amount of loft on the face of a driver – or any other club, for that matter.

For a driver, the loft can vary between 8 and 12 degrees. But club manufacturers know full well that most golfers would find an 8-degree loft difficult or even impossible. Any player, however accomplished, who draws the ball, or has his hands well forward of the clubhead at impact might well find this to be the case.

So manufacturers tend to produce far more drivers with lofts at the top end of the range. What you are getting, you might say, isn't a driver at all, but something much more like a 2-wood. You have a club which can easily get the ball airborne for you from a reasonable fairway lie.

HOW MANY WOODS?

The rules of golf limit us to 14 clubs. It is up to each individual golfer to decide on the combination which is best.

Most players, for example, find that on any average day, they are better with woods than they are with irons – or vice versa. This gives a clear choice – is it better to try to improve a weakness or to play to one's strength?

The great Hungarian soccer player, Ferenc Puskas provides an example of one solution to this dilemma. He was said to have 'no right foot', a charge which worried the roly-poly Hungarian not in the least. He concentrated his practice on honing his skills and developing his power with the left.

You could take a leaf from the Puskas book if, for example, your strength lies in the long irons. Many tournament players make only limited use of their woods, even from the tee. If they can crack a 1-iron more than 250 yards, they might not carry a fairway wood at all. They might occasionally use a driver from the fairway, and don't miss the extra distance which a fairway wood would give them.

But these are superb strikers of the ball, with very fast hands – both essentials for consistent long hitting with a 1-iron. For the average player, the 1-iron is the most difficult club of all to use, and off-centre strikes do not travel nearly as far as the same amount of error would give you when using a wood. The poor long iron player will almost certainly score better by making more use of woods.

The standard set of woods on offer at your pro shop will be driver, 3 and 4, or driver, 3 and 5, but this comes nowhere near representing the choice available.

I once played golf with a man who had no irons in his bag at all, except a blade putter. Admittedly, he was an exceptional case; a man who had been driven to give up the game, at one time, by intolerable shanking. Then a friend told him that you could buy a complete set of clubs, all of which were woods, and he was soon happily pitching away with a short-shafted wood bearing the number '10' on the sole plate, and so on, back through the set to the driver.

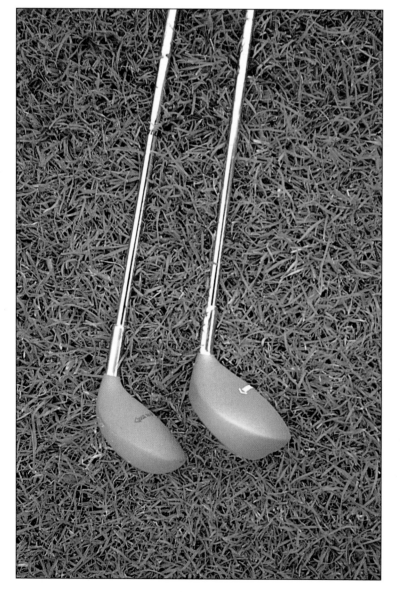

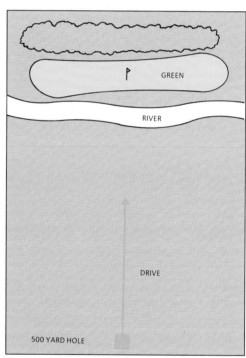

ABOVE: A long approach to a narrow green such as this requires a high-flighted shot if the ball is to clear the stream and stop quickly without running into the trees behind.

LEFT: A metal-headed driver and a 5-wood – both have their uses off the tee and on the fairway. Note the small head of the latter.

ABOVE: A long fairway wood shot. The green is in the centre.

Not that I'm suggesting you do the same. My playing partner lacked precision from, say, 100 yards in. His woods gave him limited backspin, and even with his 10-wood, he sometimes hit the ball much too far – perhaps when he got his hands well ahead of the clubhead at impact, and therefore de-lofted the club.

There are, however, far less extreme options worth your consideration, which involve dropping only the long irons from your set. You might carry a driver for your tee shots, and a 3- or 4-wood for length from the fairway.

Now, we are in the area of substituting woods for irons. Let's take a look at the various uses of the 5-wood and start with an example.

One of the most dominant performances ever seen at the US Masters was the display put on by Raymond Floyd in 1976. He opened up with rounds of 65 and 66, and eventually cruised home by eight strokes; this in an event which seems to produce more close finishes and play-offs than most.

Sales of the 5-wood soared in the USA. Why?

Simply because Floyd had given considerable thought to which clubs he would carry in that year's Masters, giving close attention to how Augusta's par 5's should be played. He decided that high flight to the greens on these holes was important, because he needed, not only to hit the greens, but hold them as well. His 1-iron had to go. Instead, he chose to carry a 5-wood for the shape of shot it gave him.

The result was that Floyd played the 5's at Augusta just about as well as they have ever been played in competition. He was 13 under par for these holes!

Club golfers took note of this object lesson, at least for a while, and indeed, the benefits can be substantial. 5-woods give height, good length, and more important, are easy to play. The shorter shaft helps control, and the extra loft undoubtedly cuts down the effects of hook and draw spin.

It is often said that the 5-wood's main advantages become apparent from the rough, when the small head pushes easily through the grass, and the loft gets the ball airborne quickly. Neither of these factors matter in the least from the fairway.

Here, there are two major uses. You can expect greater accuracy to place a second shot exactly where you want it at a par 5, and for shots to the greens you get Ray Floyd's advantage of high flight which helps to hold the greens. This is especially useful if there are water hazards, or bunkers, close to the green and between you and the flag: you can hit over them without incurring the excessive run you'll get from a long iron.

BELOW: If you are coming in over this water hazard you need a high shot to clear it and hold the green beyond – a 5-wood might be the solution from some distance out.

There are other 'utility' woods which are worth considering, although you won't find them in every pro shop. As you'd expect, the most common are the 6 and 7. Depending on the swing characteristics of individual players, these two cover distances roughly equivalent to those given by 3- to 5-irons. From the fairway, their benefits are just about the same as those of the 5-wood, except, of course, for reduced length and higher flight.

3- AND 4-WOODS

There is so little difference in the usefulness of these two woods that it is not worth separating them. Unlike the 4- and 5-irons, we seldom use these woods where the slight difference in length will be significant.

Imagine you are trying to hit a far-distant green. Your success or otherwise will be decided by the quality of your strike, and whether you were right to select a wood in the first place, than by which of these two woods you decided to use.

It's a bit extravagant to have both of these woods in your bag. In any case, you will tend to use the one in which you have more confidence. It would be better, therefore, to discard the less-favoured club and replace it with a second pitching wedge, with more loft than your usual one.

My general advice would be to stay with a 3-wood if you cut the ball. In that case, you need the extra length which this club gives you, and you should have no problem getting your shots off the ground. If you tend to draw the ball, the reverse advice would apply. The 4-wood will work better, because you probably tend to take some loft from the clubface, and consequently smother a proportion of your shots.

Playing either club is just the same as using a driver from the fairway – but easier. The shorter shafts aid control of the clubhead, and the extra loft lessens slice or hook spin.

The smaller heads are also useful when the ball finds a fluffy lie – a patch where the mowers haven't cut quite as closely as elsewhere. Much the same is true when the lie is bare of grass. In this case, although an iron might still be the club to play, the way the clubhead of a fairway wood sits to the ball gives more confidence than a driver head would. This can be the constant situation on the sort of tight lies found on links courses.

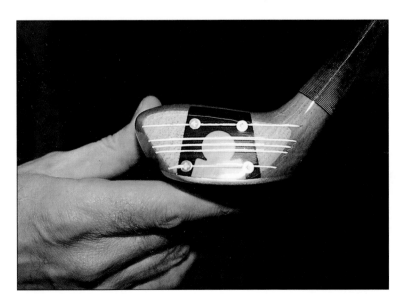

LEFT: A 3-wood – the shorter shaft and greater degree of loft makes it easier to play from the fairway than a longer-shafted and flatter-faced driver.

ABOVE AND RIGHT: The address and early stages of the backswing when playing a 3-wood from a slightly fluffy lie on the fairway. Note the position of the ball in relation to the golfer's left heel. It is slightly further back in the stance than it would be if this shot were being played from a flatter lie. This helps to minimize the risk of trapping grass between the club face and ball just before impact. Note also the smooth take away and the shoulders beginning to turn.

ABOVE AND LEFT: At the top, the downswing and the finish. Note the full shoulder turn at the top, the return to a square position just before impact and the high finish – all indicating that the golfer has hit powerfully through the ball in an effort to ensure elevation, length and accuracy.

A 3-wood from a better lie this time, and the ball is slightly further forward in the stance.

Having checked his line the golfer addresses the ball.

A smooth take away, and no sign of the wrists breaking at this stage.

The wrists just begin to break

The wrist continue to break as the shoulders begin to turn.

The shoulders nearly at full turn as the golfer approaches the top of the backswing.

Well into the downswing now, with the wrists still cocked and the shoulders coming back to a square-on position.

Finally, through the ball with the shoulders and hips completing a full turn to ensure length and accuracy.

THE IRONS

'Only God can hit a 1-iron.' This is one of the whole series of golfing *bon mots* invented by Lee Trevino – or, the uncharitable would suggest, his script writer – over the years. There may be some justification for it, but it has become less true over the years.

What Lee had in mind, was the fact that the 1-iron *used* to be a very difficult club to play consistently, and perhaps the most unforgiving club in the bag. Many – perhaps the majority of – tournament players preferred not to play the club, stopping short at the 2-iron, or perhaps the 3-iron, substituting an extra wood. This was even more true of club players. 20 or 30 years ago, very few carried a 1-iron.

All golfers face the same problem to some degree. In terms of lost distance, it was a very unforgiving club when the player missed the 'sweet spot', compared with the effect of an off-centre shot with a wooden club. The actual distance lost from a pure or merely so-so strike with a wood is often remarkably little.

Things were quite different with a 1-iron. A poor strike seemed to get you nowhere at all, and the club found very little favour for tee shots. Lack of loft meant, and still means, that spin imparted by an inadvertent slice or hook makes the ball swing far more wildly, left or right, than is the case when the same shot is hit with, say a 4-wood.

Highly accomplished players welcome this. If you have the ability to bend the ball either way at will, the straight face of a 1-iron will enhance this skill, and improve your chances of bringing off the desired shot.

Nowadays, perimeter weighting on so many clubs has greatly reduced the terrors of the 1-iron. This type of clubhead design ensures that the off-centre shot isn't punished by loss of distance to anything like the same degree. The ability to use the club no longer belongs to the Almighty alone.

In recent years, the most renowned user of the 1-iron has probably been Sandy Lyle. One of the game's most

LEFT The key to playing a good shot with a 1-iron is to swing smoothly. At address the ball is positioned two to three inches inside the left heel.

RIGHT: As you take the club back, don't be tempted to break the wrists too early.

LEFT AND RIGHT: The wrists should begin to break at or just before waist-height – as the shoulders begin to turn.

LEFT: At the top of the swing the shoulders have reached full-turn and the shaft is not quite parallel to the ground. **RIGHT AND BELOW:** Just after impact, and the player is swinging smoothly through the ball to ensure a good turn and a high finish.

powerful players, he makes little use of the driver during an average round, getting all the length he needs from his 1-iron – 260 yards plus – and he feels far more confident of keeping his ball on the fairway.

We, however, would probably do better to avoid thinking of using this club for great distance. Such a train of thought quite often leads to the use of excessive force. Better to behave as you would with a 5-iron in your hands: use a full swing, but think rhythm, balance and precision.

THE LONG IRONS

We have considered the 1-iron separately, because, unarguably one of the long irons, it is still a specialist club. The remainder (2 through 4), entail no significant difference in the way they are played. The stance and the swing both remain unaltered.

But beware of that word 'long'. It does suggest, don't you think, that you are supposed to hit a long way with them. This often persuades golfers to lash at the ball.

ABOVE: The peripheral weighting incorporated into the head of this 1-iron has enlarged the sweet spot and made it more forgiving of the less-than-perfect strike.

BELOW: Just as you would with any other club, adopt a comfortable address position with a long iron and don't try to belt the ball a long distance.

Remember, that these irons are merely clubs designed to vary the distance the ball travels. When considering your shot, your attitude should be exactly the same as when you are playing, say, a 7-iron. Your aim is to hit a target, and you choose a club which will give you the required length. Having done that – go ahead. Use your normal swing speed, thinking precision, rather than striving for maximum distance.

It will do no harm at all if you can maintain the same attitude as when you are playing a full pitch. Although you should swing at high speed, about 20 per cent of your capacity should remain unused.

RIGHT: Having selected the long iron, line up square to the target and make sure you aren't standing too close to the ball.

RIGHT: Take the club back square to, and as the shoulders turn, inside the line.

RIGHT: At the top of the swing the club should be pointing towards the target.

RIGHT: Pull the club back down inside the line, with the shoulders returning to a square-on position.

RIGHT: Let the momentum of the swing uncock the wrists,

RIGHT: . . . and at impact drive smoothly through with the right arm and shoulder – but don't force the shot.

RIGHT: Turn the shoulders and hips and produce a high finish.

Again, a comfortable address position.

A smooth, one-piece take away.

Wrists break and shoulders begin to turn.

Back nearly square-on to the target.

Club slightly over the parallel this time.

Keeping inside the line and not stretching for the ball.

Accelerating into impact.

Driving legs, hand, arms and shoulders through the ball. . .

to produce a full turn and a high finish.

THE MID-IRONS

As the term implies, these are clubs around the middle of the range; the 5-, 6- and 7-irons. Many club professionals, giving lessons to beginners, start their pupils off using one of these clubs. They are the easiest to use, the shafts are not long (which helps), and lofts are not extreme in either direction. Pupils, it is hoped, won't be discouraged by hitting a series of unsuccessful shots.

Mid-irons should be played with a square stance, and a ball position approximately inside the left heel. The only difference from swinging a long iron is that the shorter shafts lead to a more upright swing plane.

You may well find that one of these clubs – the 6-iron is probably the most likely candidate – becomes the one in which you have the most confidence from your whole set. If this proves to be the case, you can capitalize by making extra use of it.

The 6-iron, for example, gives quite good length, and can be used for this purpose for second shots on a par 5 from poor fairway lies, or when the ball isn't sitting up in the semi-rough. Used well below full power, the club can also be useful for pitching, particularly to soft, holding greens.

Here the player has to clear some trees and a bunker to reach the green.

A mid-iron will give him the necessary loft, and a smooth, one-piece take away gives him a good start.

Because of the shorter shaft length, the wrists will break slightly earlier with a mid-iron than a long iron.

The player could have stopped here before beginning his downswing . . .

but he went just over the parallel.

A good position as the club head returns to the ball.

At impact.

Well through the ball now.

And a good finish, with the hands above
head height.

Playing a 6-iron from the fairway.

The 6-iron is one of the most versatile and
easiest of clubs to play.

ABOVE: A mid-iron this time, but you should adopt the same approach as for a long iron – although the shorter shaft length will mean that you will be standing slightly shorter and a bit closer to the ball.

ABOVE RIGHT: Again, note the one-piece take away – the left arm straight and the wrists unbroken.

LEFT: Although the overall position is good at the top of the swing, the club has gone over the parallel. This can lead to a loss of control on the downswing and shouldn't be necessary with a mid-iron.

RIGHT: Again, this is a position as the swing nears completion. The head, shoulders, chest and hips have been driven almost square to the target by the fluid momentum of the swing.

RIGHT: The right heel high off the ground, high hands and the club around the back of the neck mark the finish of a full and well-struck mid-iron.

CHAPTER THREE

THE SHORT PITCH

Today, the word 'chip' is quite often used to refer to what I, and many others, would call a 'pitch'. This is particularly true when the shot in question is, in fact, a short pitch, so perhaps I'd better define my terms.

The short pitch is, quite simply, a shot which the golfer visualizes, and hopes to play, mainly through the air. Even over very short distances, it will rise quite high, and has little run.

RIGHT: A poor pitch from here and you would end up in the water hazard!

Just off the green and a chip with a short iron . . .

. . . gets the ball into the air and onto the putting surface.

With humpy ground between you and the green . . .

. . . you must pitch over it to get to the flag.

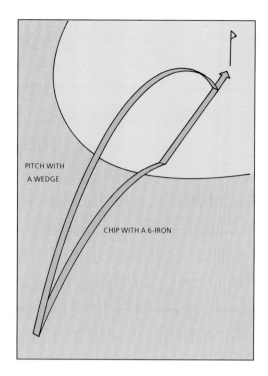

ABOVE: From the same position off the green, a pitch with a wedge will have a higher trajectory. and will land closer to the flag and stop quicker than an equivalent chip with a 6-iron.

In this sense, a short pitch may be played only a few yards from the flag – over a greenside bunker, perhaps, to a flag set close by. If you played a chip, which is a low, running shot, you'd finish in the sand under your nose, or run on well past the flag.

Though this is a situation where a cut-up shot has to be played, the necessity for taking that sort of risk rapidly decreases when the flag isn't quite as close. Now, we are in the territory of the short pitch.

This is played in a straightforward manner, without any need to open the face and cut across the line of flight.

But it still isn't simple, perhaps because many golfers are uncomfortable when employing a half or three-quarter swing. There are two pitfalls to avoid:

(1) Don't take a short backswing, and then push your hands into the shot, at the last moment, to make up for the loss of pace which your too-short backswing has landed you with.

(2) If your backswing *is* long enough – even too long, perhaps – don't decelerate into the ball.

As you can see, these are opposite hazards, and they indicate that a major difficulty of the very short pitch is feel and control of length, pace and rhythm of your swing.

Set up with your shoulders parallel to the target line, and with the ball, either opposite the left heel, or just slightly further back in your stance. For a start, play with your feet parallel, too, but you may, after practice, find it easier to play with your left foot a couple of inches withdrawn. This gives more freedom to swing hands and arms through, but if you find you're cutting across the ball, then you should revert to a wholly square stance.

RIGHT: A slightly open stance for a short pitch.

Setting up for a full pitch.

Feet square to the line and the ball inside the left heel.

Take the club back smoothly – don't 'pick it up' with the hands.

Shoulder beginning to turn.

A three-quarter swing takes you to the top.

Halfway down and the shoulders are squaring up again.

The momentum of the swing gives
you a high finish.

Assessing the results.

To clear this bunker and get the ball
close to the flag . . .

. . . all that's needed is a short, firm
swing (not a jab) . . .

In this shot, exact striking means a great deal, in terms
of both distance and trajectory. Help yourself to achieve this
by gripping down towards the bottom of the handle.

The length of your backswing will depend on the
distance required, and the club you have selected.
But remember – it should never be very short, because that
would invariably lead to a jab rather than a swinging
movement. Not less than waist high, and not often much
more than shoulder height are useful rules of thumb.

Think of the shot as one played by arms and shoulders,
with the wrists only breaking on rather longer pitch shots.
Otherwise, the hands should be kept out of this shot as much
as possible. This way, you eliminate the danger of letting the
clubhead get ahead of the hands which is one of the prime
causes of inconsistency.

. . . to produce a near-perfect result.

As with long and mid-irons, a full pitch to a green, demands . . .   . . . a smooth, one-piece take away . . .

. . . a full turn of the shoulders . . .   . . . taking the club to either just short of parallel to the ground . . .

... or parallel – and on line with the target ...

... before bringing it back down inside the line ...

... and hitting through the ball ...

... to a high finish.

Don't be tempted to lift your head early . . .

. . . or you'll top it into the trees.

A typical shot from the fairway.

When you are in good form, you may just be able to get away with this, but you won't succeed week-in and week-out.

Visualize what happens when the clubhead does get ahead of the hands. The amount by which this occurs is certain to vary. The loft of your club effectively changes, the amount of height achieve varies, and it becomes quite impossible to be consistent

The shorter the pitch shot, the more useful it is to use your putting grip. This is especially true if you keep your wrists out of your putting stroke. Let me give you an example: like many other great players, Jack Nicklaus has been accused of being 'finished' at various times in his career. Curtis Strange, Tom Watson, Sandy Lyle and Seve Ballesteros had the same accusation levelled at them in the 1990 season. Hale Irwin was definitely thought of as a figure of the past – until he won the 1990 US Open. We just never know, until we have the advantage of the perspective of history.

Jack Nicklaus first faced this judgement towards the end of the 1960s. He had been enormously successful, but his record began to decline in major championships. The talking stopped when he won the 1970 British Open.

All went well until 1979, when Jack had a bad year in all kinds of competition. By now, he was on the verge of his 40th birthday, so perhaps there was more justification for supposing his career at the top was over. Although he had lost some length, he felt that his major weakness was in his short game, which had never been a strong feature. His putting, however, had always been very good indeed.

Jack then took on short-game expert, Phil Rodgers, as coach, principally to improve the range and precision of his shots around the green. Rodgers taught him a lot, and suggested, among other things, that he use his conventional reverse overlap putting grip for short pitching and chipping.

In 1980, Nicklaus became one of the few men to win two majors in a year – the US Open and US PGA.

I don't suggest, for a moment, that this technique will revolutionize your game, but it could help you to feel that the short pitch is a shot played with arms and shoulders, rather than with a wristy flick.

Many beginners, and even advanced, players feel that the short pitch shot is the weakest part of their game. The two prime reasons for this are the necessity for exact length and for very good, consistent striking. The angle of loft of the pitching club must remain constant if an identical result from the same swing speed is to be achieved. It is worth persistent practice to ensure that the hands are always ahead of the clubhead at impact, and that the *amount* by which they are ahead is constant.

When this varies, you are, in effect, using the angle of loft of, say, a wedge for one shot, followed by an 8- or perhaps

RIGHT: The results of two fine pitches to the green.

If you have a good lie . . .

. . . a short pitch with a sand wedge . . .

. . . will give you more height than with a
pitching wedge . . .

. . . and allow you to stop the ball quickly on
the green.

a sand iron next time. No one can possibly be a consistent short pitcher if they are 'flippy wristed'.

As with long putting, distance is more important than direction when pitching. Imagine that your ball has been pitched three yards too far. The difference is negligible if your shot was directly over the flag or was a yard or two either side However, it certainly matters if you are always getting your distance right, but are consistently wide of the hole.

To improve your direction, take just as much care when setting up to square your clubface along the target line as you would if you were putting. Many tend to let nature do the job for them, but that's usually not good enough. If your hand position is consistent, that should do the job for you.

CLUB SELECTION FOR THE SHORT PITCH

Although the short pich is, by definition, a short shot, there is still a range of possibilities when selecting a club. The sand iron is probably the most effective choice from good lies, because a ball which stops quickly from such a gentle strike will do so because of its height, not from backspin. However, the extreme loft of the club makes it a little more difficult to achieve consistency. Most people will probably find that the wedge will give a better average result.

When you have sufficient green to play with, a 9-iron, or perhaps the 8-iron can be used. They are easier clubs with which to achieve consistent distance through the air, and it's easy to learn to adjust for the greater run which results from the less extreme lofts.

THE MEDIUM PITCH

Here, we are talking about marginal differences. The short pitch is played with a mini-swing, while the medium pitch simply means you take a longer swing – about three-quarters – while making your strike considerably firmer.

As the medium pitch needs far less feel, it is, hopefully, easier to play. Penalties for an imprecise strike are less severe, because we don't really expect to lay this shot dead by the side of the hole.

THE FULL PITCH

So far, I've not mentioned distance, and said very little about club selection. These omissions are deliberate: all pitches are simply shots which travel along a high trajectory, and run

For a very short pitch, open the blade of the club to the line of the shot . . .

. . . minimize wrist movement during the short backswing . . .

. . . and hit firmly through the ball.

LEFT TO RIGHT, TOP TO BOTTOM: For a medium length pitch again, make a one-piece take away and don't take more than a three-quarter length swing. Strike the ball firmly all the while concentrating on the length of the shot.

Take a full backswing for a full-length pitch.

From top to bottom, the different trajectories of a sand wedge, a wedge, a 9-iron, an 8-iron and a 5-iron.

along the ground for a relatively short distance. It therefore doesn't matter what number is inscribed on your club. Trajectory and run are what counts.

But there are limits. A searing 1-iron which seriously incommodes a butterfly alighting on a buttercup is obviously no pitch. We might well draw a line at a club with the maximum loft of a 5-iron, and then only if the player naturally gets a high flight from his shots.

Normally, we think of the pitching clubs as 8- through sand iron, as the up-and-down flight of the pitch shades into a more shallow arc, roughly from this point.

Whatever the club, however, the full pitch remains basically the same shot, but played with a full swing of the club. But do remember that it is a precision shot, and that your swing should always be under complete control. Keep a measured pace, and never lash at the ball. Try to ignore the golfer who delights in hitting his pitching clubs the maximum distance he can wring out of them, and then crows about getting 'up with a drive and a 9-iron . There are no prizes for how far you hit a pitch. What counts is how close you get to the hole.

To help you remember this, and also to assist your control, grip one or two inches down the shaft.

Addressing the ball with an 8-iron.

As with the other irons, making a one-piece take away.

Nearing the top of the swing.

At the top of the swing for a full 8-iron shot.

Swinging through the ball.

Once again, to a high finish.

LEFT: Addressing the ball with a pitching wedge.

RIGHT: Wrist beginning to break after a one-piece take away.

LEFT: At the top of the swing for a full shot.

RIGHT: Hitting firmly through the ball.

LEFT: Nearing the top of the swing.

RIGHT: A full turn, and the ball's on its way to the flag.

RIGHT: Positioning the ball opposite the right heel for a low-flying sand wedge.

THE LOW SAND IRON (WEDGE)

The most remarkable golfer to emerge immediately following World War II was Bobby Locke. His technique in the long game was highly unorthodox: he had a great loop in his backswing, went right out of plane at the top of it, and his left wrist was anything but firm. But he had great feel for his swing, and found the fairway very consistently.

His legendary strengths were in his short game. Locke's putting was a source of wonder, and his abilities with the short irons were superb. Again, his feel for his swing and judgement of distance seemed to guarantee that, even if he was occasionally a little off line, he was invariably pin high.

One of his specialities was the use of the low-flying wedge, which he played with a broad-soled club of his own design, broadly similar to a conventional sand iron, with the mass of clubhead weight right at the sole.

In contrast, today's conventional wedge is often far more similar to a 9-iron with extra loft. In other words, it's a 10-iron, and is sometimes numbered as such.

Playing this club demands a change in your usual set up. The ball is positioned approximately opposite your right heel,

LEFT TO RIGHT, TOP TO BOTTOM: Playing a low sand iron. Here the stance is less extreme than this club normally requires, and the backswing is slightly too high.

and the toe of the club is turned in. This is to compensate for the tendency of the blade to open at address, owing to the ball's position, so unusually far back in your stance.

The hands should fall naturally into position, well ahead of your clubhead, which is precisely where you want them to be, at address and impact. The backswing should be comparatively short, perhaps not much more than waist high, and the wrists should be kept firm throughout. However, it is important to avoid too short a backswing.

The action into the ball is very much a pull, with no wrist movement whatsoever. You should have the feeling that you are pulling the ball towards the flag, rather than striking it towards the target.

Your swing will be very much down at the ball, on a steep arc, producing extreme backspin, with the ball being squeezed between clubhead and turf.

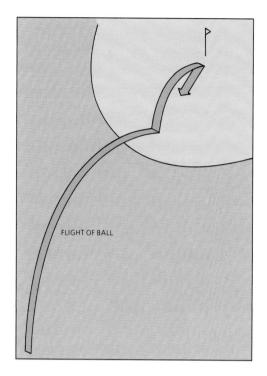

ABOVE: The considerable backspin imparted by a low-flying wedge shot takes effect on the second bounce of the ball, and will bring it to an abrupt halt or, on some occasions, roll it back towards you.

BELOW: When your ball is up against a collar of rough, thinning it with the leading edge of a wedge will get you out of trouble.

There are various advantages to this shot, not least the benefits you will obtain in strong winds. Whatever the wind direction, the effect on the ball will be minimal, because the low flight of the ball keeps it well below the wind's main strength. When playing into a gale, a high pitch shot simply can't be judged: your ball may even be blown back towards you. If the wind is behind you, much backspin is taken off once it gets up into the air.

Of course, there will still be some effect from the wind, just as there is when playing the putt, which is the lowest shot of all, but it will be minimized, and experience will enable you to make allowances much more easily than you can for high shots.

One thing you'll relish is that this shot, well played, is spectacular. Low flight, combined with speed through the air, makes it seem certain that your ball will finish many yards beyond the hole. The first bounce does nothing at all to change that impression. But when the ball makes contact with the ground for the second time, the extreme backspin really takes effect, and the ball stops dead – perhaps even spins back towards you.

Other advantages of the shot include the extra confidence it will give you when playing from a bare lie. Unless your sand iron has a very low trailing edge, that advanced hand position will make you feel very confident of good ball contact.

It's quite possible to make this shot your standard method on short approach, but there are drawbacks to it. When greens are variable it doesn't work at all consistently. Remember that the professionals you see in tournaments derive remarkable backspin because the greens they are playing on are in peak condition. However closely they are cut, and however fast they putt, grass growth is very dense, which greatly helps the ball's backspin to grip the putting surface.

You won't get consistent results when this isn't so. Neither will you when greens through a round of golf vary from soft to firm.

THE THINNED WEDGE

Golfers afflicted with problems on the greens have used just about every club in the bag, with the exception of the lofted irons, for putting. My 'thinned wedge' is really a specialized kind of putt.

Quite often, during a golfing year, your ball will come to rest just off the green, resting either against the beginning of the fringe of the green, or a little further on – on the fringe and against longer grass beyond. Whether you decide to chip or putt, the problem is the same – even though you may bring your club quite steeply down on the ball, blades of grass will intrude.

This is where our thinned wedge comes in. Address the ball with the leading edge of your club aligned against the equator of the ball. Your gentle strike should not be impeded by grass, but it must still be precise. If you make contact just below the equator, your ball will hop, rather than run, and you won't get the distance you anticipated. If contact is made much above the equator, you have a topped shot and, again, less distance.

An exact strike will give you a running ball like a putt, but beware – this shot *must* be practised. You will have no confidence at all if you suddenly try to use it in a competitive situation, with no previous experience.

THE CUT-UP SHOT

Often known as the 'lob', this is a difficult shot, and should only be used by golfers of average ability when full of confidence, or perhaps as an all-or-nothing shot in matchplay.

The aim of the shot, played with a sand iron or wedge, is to put maximum height on a very short pitch, so that there will be little forward momentum on the ball when it pitches on the green. Height, as well as backspin, often decides how much run there will be on the ball.

It is most useful when playing to a green on a higher level than you are, or when playing over an obstacle – a bunker perhaps – when the flag is close beyond it.

Set up with an open stance, with the ball opposite your left instep. With your body aligned to the left of your target, aim the club face at the hole, or a little left, if you expect some side spin. Lift the club sharply, as though for a bunker shot, and then swing across the target line, getting the feeling of sliding your club under the ball.

This shot is easiest to play when your ball is on a slight upslope, or is, at least, cushioned by a layer of grass on the flat.

Don't attempt to play it when you have:
(1) A downhill lie.
(2) A bare, or hardpan, lie.
(3) Not practised the shot.
(4) No confidence in your ability to play it.

A lot can go wrong with this shot. I've seen Tom Watson, one of the masters of the lob, shank when he brought the heel of the club in flrst. However, a more likely fault is inexactness in sliding your clubhead into the ball. The result is likely to be a thinned shot, treating you to the sight of your ball scuttling

ABOVE: A cut-up shot will get the ball up into the air very quickly and land it on the green with little forward momentum.

BELOW: Cutting across the ball results in a high trajectory, and imparts backspin and sidespin – both of which take effect when the ball lands on the green.

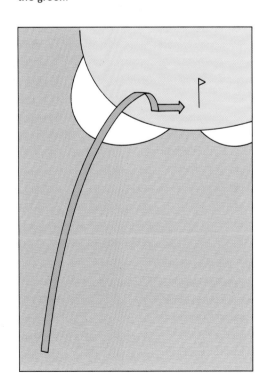

RIGHT: A classic situation – and one that calls for the cut-up shot.

RIGHT AND FAR RIGHT: Here we see the cut-up shot applied to good effect.

through the green, rather than landing, as Lee Trevino puts it, as lightly as 'a butterfly with sore feet.

Elsewhere, I have remarked that a sand iron should have a trailing edge lower than its leading edge. If you have one do not attempt to use it for the cut up shot, unless the lie is well grassed. That trailing edge is likely to catch the ground first, resulting in a bounce and the leading edge thinning the ball. Stick to your wedge. The more lofted, the better.

Although you don't need a full backswing, this should be a flowing shot, with swing energy expended in hitting the ball upward, rather than forward. Very precise contact is needed, because the club moves sharply across the ball. But when it comes off – it's a delight.

WHY NOT THREE WEDGES?

Tom Kite is 5 feet 8 inches tall, and although 'mighty atoms' such as Ian Woosnam tend to disprove the rule, lack of height tends to mean short driving. Indeed Tom Kite is, by today's standards, by no means a long hitter, but he's among the most prolific of all money winners. Only his repeated failures to win major tournaments tarnish his reputation, and deny him his ranking among the greatest players.

Length from the tee is vital for Tour players, mainly because of the advantages which follow for playing the shot to the green. Just like club players, they are more accurate with short irons than long. This has given Kite an inbuilt disadvantage when compared with his fellow competitors when playing long 4's and par 5's. One way he can redress the balance is through his putting and his short game.

Early in the 1980s, Kite decided to abandon his 2-iron. To compensate for this at one end of the iron range, he had the lofts of his 3-, 4- and 5- changed, to fill in the gaps partially. Now he was free to carry three wedges – a sand iron, a 'strong' wedge and a 'weak' one.

This is a thought I commend to club golfers. Many of us are far more comfortable playing either full shots or little ones, but far less happy with anything in between. By this, I mean something of the order of half swing power.

Perhaps, to some extent, Tom felt the same. His strong and weak wedges gave him the opportunity to play relatively full shots with his three wedges, rather than have to play so many half power shots. He had a great money-winning year immediately afterwards, and many more since.

Golfers weren't restricted to 14 clubs until the late 1930s. In any case, in earlier years, no one even thought of carrying such a vast quantity. Open Champions around the turn of the century regarded 7 to 10 clubs as the norm. Between the wars, all this changed dramatically.

Rightly or wrongly, top professionals decided that it is far more difficult to be consistent when you have to vary your swing pace, and alter your clubface position at impact by manipulating it with the hands. They felt it was far easier to repeat a standard full swing. Some of them began to carry, not 14 clubs, but quantities soaring into the 20's.

Lawson Little, still the only player to win the Amateur Championships of both Britain and the USA in two consecutive years, was known for carrying a positive battery of pitching clubs. He would smash the ball vast distances from the tee, and then select a suitable club for 60, 85, 100 yards, and so on. Craig Wood was another power player with much the same approach. So was Walter Hagen, strange though it may seem for a player who relied on touch, rather than power.

Hagen's motives were different. He didn't actually carry his 25 clubs to use, but because he was paid a fee by a manufacturer which varied according to the number of clubs he carried. Being a logical thinker, Hagen stuffed his bag full of clubs, and held out his hand for the cheque.

We live in different times now. You could say that a full set of clubs to include most of the standard ones is 16 – four woods, 11 irons and a putter. It is up to the golfer to decide which are the most useful.

Many consider a couple of woods to be enough for their needs, and that the 1- and 2-irons are too difficult to use anyway. If you think this way, then you have already knocked four clubs out of that standard manufactured set of 16.

You already have one wedge and a sand iron, so you have room, under the Rules of Golf, not for one extra wedge but *two*.

Give it a thought.

THE BASIC CHIP SHOT

You'll sometimes hear a fellow golfer say, 'I chipped in from 100 yards.' All that proves is that he doesn't understand golf language.

I'll start by making the definitions of these terms quite clear, and by describing the differences between a chip and a pitch – which is what your fellow golfer must have been talking about.

A good chip and it's nearly stone dead.

LEFT: From this position you can either play a pitch or a chip.

RIGHT: The golfer addresses his ball . . .

LEFT: and takes the club back.

RIGHT: The ball rapidly gains height, revealing this to be a pitch and not a chip.

LEFT: The ball pitches on the playing surface . . .

RIGHT: . . . and runs up to the flag.

The differences are simple enough. The pitch travels mainly through the air, usually running for quite a short proportion of its total distance. The chip, on the other hand, is really a close relative of the putt. You should see it as a shot which mainly runs towards the flag, only the first part of its journey being through the air.

The shot is usually played from not more than a few yards of the putting surface, the basic idea being that the second or two of flight is enough to carry the ball to the putting surface. It then runs the rest of the way to the flag. Once you are further away from the green, and using more swing speed, the shot becomes more like a pitch. It will fly further through the air, because of the loft of the club, and greater momentum will impart more backspin and cause the ball to fly. It's really something halfway between a pitch and a chip. You could call it a running pitch.

The chip shot can be played with any iron in the bag, although anything more straight-faced than a 4-iron is seldom used. It's a specialized stroke, so it's wise to emulate the professionals and use very few of your clubs. In this way, you can become more accustomed to the feel of the clubs, and the way the ball responds in this very gentle stroke.

Some professionals prefer to hone their skills with just one chipping club. This probably would be a wedge, but possibly could be a 9- or sand iron.

As these are the most lofted clubs in the bag, it may be a puzzle as to why the ball runs rather than climbs into the air. The answer is that this is a gentle shot, which means that there is little backspin to persuade the ball to climb.

Far more important are the various techniques used for playing the shot. There are similarities with the putt, one important one being that there is little or no use of the wrists.

You get the feeling that you are swinging the arms back and through, getting your pace from this mini-swing, not from use of hands and wrists. You will find that, if you allow the wrists to flex, the ball will usually climb, and that your strike will become less consistent.

The length of shot determines how far you should take the club back, so there can be no firm rule about it. However, you are not flexing the wrists, so the backswing should be longer than you might at first think. Watch the professionals. Even when playing from just off the green, with the flag just a few yards away, the swing is by no means restricted to just a few inches: indeed, it looks capable of sending the ball a good many yards.

It doesn't, because they have taken the hands out of the stroke, and swing gently, though still firmly. But beware of swinging too far, and then decelerating into the ball. As with any shot, even when tapping the ball into the hole from two inches, the strike must be decisive.

ABOVE: Playing out under the branches of the trees calls for a long-running chip shot.

BELOW: The different trajectories of a chip shot played with a wedge, 8-iron, 6-iron and 4-iron.

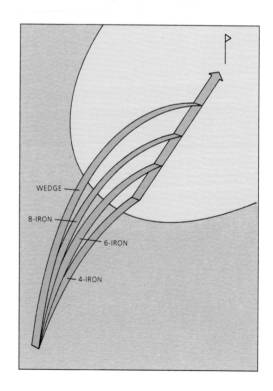

OPPOSITE (TOP TO BOTTOM): In this situation you could play a wedge, a 4-iron or a putter.

STANCE

This isn't a full swing shot, so it helps to have the hips out of the way before you start, allowing your arms to swing through much more freely. Do this by taking up a slightly open stance.

Many players like to grip the club fairly well down, making the length of the club closer to that of a putter, and also enabling them to strike down a little more firmly – the longer the shaft, the longer the potential shot.

A shorter grip means that the ball will be lying closer to the feet, creating a situation closer to a putt, and getting your eyes more nearly over the ball.

So the ball is fairly close to the line of your feet, but you now have to decide how far forward or back in your stance it ought to be. The extremes are from inside the left heel to inside the right. Any further can lead to problems: too far forward and you may hit on the upswing, too far back and the swing down becomes too steep.

But there can be no firm rule, because much depends on the position of the hands.

ABOVE: A long chip with a 6-iron.

ABOVE : Gripping down the shaft of the 6-iron helps to develop a greater feel for distance.

HANDS

The hands must be set so that they are in front of the clubhead when it meets the ball. This means that they should reach the same position as they were in the set-up – remember, you won't be flexing those wrists.

At least, you'd better not be doing anything of the sort, because if you do, you'll have no chance of an unvarying strike. The change of the blade's loft, and the height on the blade at impact will change from chip to chip. Exact striking is even more critical here than it is in putting, and a variable hand position will dramatically change the distance your chip shots travel. Lack of consistency in this part of your stroke will also lead to chips being struck fat or thin.

Making an arms-only chipping stroke obviously removes the hands from the shot. However, they do much more than simply hold the club. It can be useful to encourage one of two feelings: either that the back of the left hand is making the stroke, or that you are bowling the ball along the ground towards the hole with your right.

There's no logical reason for it, but the left hand image usually produces a lower flight and a longer run. On the other hand, thinking of the right hand can give more feel. In either case, hold on to the feeling that the face of the club is square with the back of the left hand, or the palm of the right.

But we are aiming to take the hands out of the shot altogether, so it's equally valid not to think of the hands at all. Feel the shot through upper arms or forearms – whichever you prefer.

The golfer sets himself up for the chip . . .

. . . makes a good take away . . .

. . . strikes the ball . . .

. . . but wasn't firm enough, and the ball finishes short – never up, never in!

GRIP

As we have already seen elsewhere, in 1979 Jack Nicklaus suffered the first real slump of his career. After a remarkable competitive career that had already stretched for 20 years, to many it seemed likely that he had, at long last, reached the end of the road.

Jack Nicklaus didn't think so. He analyzed what had been happening to his game, and decided that his greatest playing weakness – his short game, little chips and pitches from close to the green – had deteriorated further.

So he went back to school and emerged with a great repertoire of short game strokes, as well as some changes of method.

One of the most noticeable of these was the change in his grip for chip shots. He began to use his reverse overlap putting grip.

That can be an incentive for anyone to give their putting grip a try when playing a chip. This is particularly true if you regard yourself as a good putter: it makes sense to stretch your strength on the greens a little further.

But there is one thing to watch out for. It's all too easy to become greedy, and having had some success with your putting grip, to use it further and further away from the green. If you remember that the reverse overlap grip isn't suitable for shots in which the wrists flex, you'll see that it won't work except for quite short shots.

The other grip is simplicity itself: simply chip with your normal grip for full shots. Only experiment and practice will teach you which of these two solutions is most likely to work for you.

WEIGHT DISTRIBUTION

Set your weight a little more on the front foot than on the rear. This helps you make a slightly downward strike at the ball, and even more important, it helps you to avoid a fatal upward flick.

CHIPPING FROM SAND

Provided that there is only a low lip facing you, a chip shot can work better than the standard splash shot, and this is particularly true when the sand is wet. However, this does need nerve: if you take any sand at all with the ball, you are left looking rather silly, because it will only have moved a couple of feet.

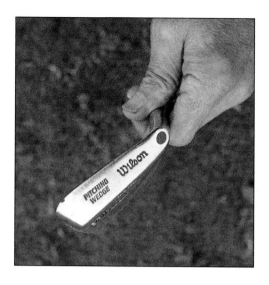

You can chip with a wedge . . .

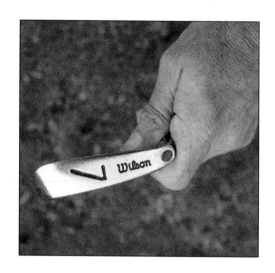

. . . a 7-iron . . .

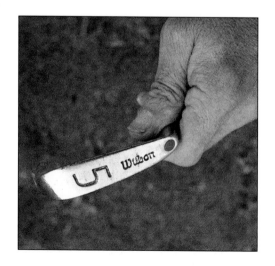

. . . or a 5-iron.

CHOICE OF CLUBS

Basically, use the clubs you feel most confident with. If you are a player who prefers to use just a single club, say a wedge, for all kinds of chip shots, you will probably be playing with your hands well ahead of the clubhead. In that case, you've taken much loft from your club, reducing it to about the loft of a 7-iron from your normal stance.

Hand position alone can be used to change the flight the club puts on the ball. Opening the blade a little gives more loft, while the opposite will happen if you hood the face. Bobby Locke preferred to confine himself to one club for chips, but by making the kind of changes just described, he could make the ball react in many different ways.

The average player won't be able to produce that range. As a result, he will benefit from letting the loft of his club vary his chipping. However, if he's going to keep his feel, it's best not to use more than three clubs.

A suitable range would be a 6-iron, an 8-iron and a wedge or sand iron. Use the 6-iron when the ball is close to the putting surface, but the flag far away, producing very little backspin and minimizing the chances of the ball gripping the turf and coming to rest earlier than you would wish. Then, use the other two clubs for progressively shorter chip shots.

Some golfers would chip from here, whilst others would putt if they are less skilled at the chip shot.

PUTT, DON'T CHIP

This may seem a negative note to end on, but it is just one way to help you make the most of your strengths.

Many club golfers think it's 'not a golf shot' to putt from more than a very few yards from the putting surface, but the pros don't think that way. They play the shots that get them the best results.

The reason that you seldom see them putting from well short of the green is that very few of them don't have great skills at chipping and short pitching. The few that don't *will* putt from many yards off, and even the others will do so occasionally, when they think they'll get a better result by putting.

A club golfer simply doesn't have that level of skills. So, if you're a good putter, but no better than average at chipping, then why not make the most of your strength? You'll be surprised at how much you can improve with more experience when putting from off the green.

You'll learn more about pace from long range, and how the ball runs over bare and rough ground. And there's one age-old truism to bear in mind: A poor putt always gets closer to the hole than a poor chip.

This golfer has decided to putt rather than chip.

The ball is on its way . . .

. . . and nears the edge of the green without being deflected . . .

. . . hits the upslope . . .

. . . and slows rapidly.

It was worth a try with the putter from there.

HITTING IT HIGH AND LOW

I was standing close to an oak tree, one day in 1990, working as a photographer at a tournament, some 40 yards short of a short par 4, reachable that day with a very good drive. A ball cracked into that tree, and came to rest.

This left a shot which demanded that the player thread his way close by the tree trunk, beneath low branches, negotiate a gap between the tree and a greenside bunker, and hopefully, find his way to the flag beyond.

RIGHT: A low chip and run is the only way out of here.

ABOVE: The green is beyond and left of centre of the big tree – a full wedge should get you there.

Closer now, and a three-quarter shot with a wedge would do it.

'Ah!' said knowledgeable father to his son, 'he'll run this one along the ground with his 5-iron.'

It seemed like a reasonable judgement. The player would have to play with touch and accuracy, and also keep his ball below the overhanging branches of the mighty oak. Then Bernhard Langer arrived. 'Sand iron', he requested caddie Peter Coleman. Was he about to waft it high over the obstacle presented by the branches? Couldn't be. They were too close.

LOW SHOTS

Langer had elected to play a low, running shot, using a sand iron rather than a 5-iron. The probable reason for this strange-seeming choice was that, like many professionals, Langer can use his sand iron to play all manner of shots. This time, he'd be keeping his hands well ahead of the clubhead to reduce the loft of the club greatly.

He swung. But his hand position wasn't what he had intended. The ball rose too high, cracked into the tree again, and came to rest only a little further forward. It was a shot wasted; Langer hadn't taken enough loft from the clubhead, and the trajectory of his shot had been much too high.

On many inland courses, trees are one of the main problems which have to be faced and dealt with. When we get out of position, through the green, they come between us and the target, so that we have to get over them, under the lower branches, or sometimes attempt to get through a gap, perhaps halfway up – very difficult, because the shot requires subtle, not extreme, variation in trajectory.

One of the easiest ways to play a low shot is to let the loft of the club do the work for you. For example, you may be a

Closer still – a cut-up shot might be called for.

Even closer, and you might have to chip under the branches from this range.

full 9-iron distance from the flag, but the loft of the club would have you clattering into that infernal tree. Instead, depending on the height of the branches, you need to choose a much straighter-faced club.

You may, perhaps, judge that you need the loft of a 3-iron, because you need very low flight. Go ahead and try it, but it's by no means easy, because you have to judge the pace of your swing (perhaps about quarter-power) and then how the ball will run. In our earlier example, Bernhard Langer almost certainly played his unsuccessful sand iron because he was confident about how the ball would behave.

A quite different approach to keeping the ball low under branches is to hood the face of your club. Set up with the ball well back in your stance, hands well ahead of the clubhead. By doing these things, you've changed the loft of, say, an 8-iron to something much closer to a 3-iron, played with a normal stance.

Swing with little or no wrist break, and keep the feeling of maintaining the hands ahead of the clubhead, while pulling through the ball. You will find the shot easier to accomplish if you also grip down the shaft.

The foregoing applies only to quite short shots, but there's no real difference for longer shots except that it isn't possible to play full swing shots with the ball set far back in your stance. All the other principles apply.

All this only applies where the grass is closely mown. Once the grass is long, you are confronted by the chance that your low shot might be killed by the long grass before it is properly airborne. In that case, you have to visualize your shot, and go for the best compromise; one which will give you the best prospect of clearing clinging grass, while also keeping below the obstacle.

From this distance you can either go over the top or underneath.

Here the branches are overhanging the player. However, the ball won't rise quickly enough to cause problems.

71

When the hands are well ahead of the ball, the clubface is hooded. Note the reduced loft of this 9-iron.

For longer shots, where maximum distance is needed, higher swing speeds mean that your ball is far more likely to rise quickly because of greater backspin. Therefore, it follows that the clubs with the least loft will work best – the driver and longest irons.

Continue to play the shot with the feeling that you are pulling the clubhead through the ball, gripping down the handle of the club, and keeping the hands ahead. Swing well within yourself, remembering that keeping the ball low is of paramount importance.

A low runner of 180 yards is a lot more rewarding than contact with those low branches.

ABOVE: The upslope will help the player to gain height on the shot.

LEFT: Not a shot for the faint-hearted!

HIGH SHOTS

Let's take that Langer oak as an example. It was near a green, and the first decision was which particular route to take?

One option, of course, is the 'low road'. Another, is to accept the likely – but not certain – loss of a shot by playing wide of the obstacle, not at the flag itself, but, perhaps, to the front or rear of the green, or perhaps a little short or long.

Or you can opt for the air route. But, if you do, you need first to be familiar with the trajectory you normally get from particular clubs, and then make a choice according to loft, and the distance you are from the obstacle.

But how to achieve more height than your norm? Naturally, you proceed with more or less reverse strategies from the ones you use when hitting the ball low. Here are some of the adjustments to make from a normal shot when maximum quick height is the aim:

(1) Place the ball further forward in your stance, but only by an inch or so. This will increase the loft of your club at impact.

(2) Open the blade slightly. This gives more loft, and promotes fade, always a higher shot than a draw.

(3) Hold the club at the end of the grip.

(4) Incorporate a lively hand action into your swing.

ABOVE: Opening the blade increases the loft of the club, and is essential if you wish to play a cut-up shot.

BELOW: Shadows across the fairway can make it difficult to assess the distance of a shot.

A high-speed cut-up shot will get the ball up into the air very quickly and over the top of this obstacle.

(5)   Hit at full swing speed. This gives maximum backspin, and your ball will climb more quickly – provided you get a good strike.

(6)   Make sure your hands aren't ahead of the clubhead at impact. But a lively hand action will probably achieve this anyway.

When your obstacle is very close, but far less high – bushes, perhaps – and the green a short distance beyond, you can achieve amazing height, but minimal length, by adding two further ingredients.

Open the blade of your club much further, and swing across the target line, much as you would for a bunker or cut-up shot. With high swing speed you will get maximum backspin, and this added to sidespin, forces nearly all the ball's momentum to be directed upwards, rather than forwards.

However, because you are pushing your techniques to the ultimate, disasters are quite likely. You could get the heel of the club into the ball, rather than the middle, and end up with a shank. If the timing is different, you may meet the ball with the toe of your club.

This is a shot with a very high skill factor, and you really shouldn't try it unless you have practised it a great deal.

RULES AND COURSE BEHAVIOUR

Thinking about course behaviour, perhaps brisk play is the best courtesy you can offer the other players in your game, and also the other users of the course.

As you walk up to your ball, be making your mind up about club selection. Consult your yardage chart, if you carry one, as you walk along.

Professionals go about their business with reasonable speed for their tee shots, because the decision is a reasonably simple one. Length of shot is often not critical. The only things they have to consider is how to be sure to be short of a fairway bunker, or that a shot down the right hand side gives a better angle for a shot to the green. Changing weather conditions can make a difference, but practice rounds have probably taught them what to do beforehand.

Approaching the greens, however, many professionals set dreadful examples for club golfers. Not only do they not decide on club selection on their way to the ball, but they

BELOW: As you walk towards your ball, start thinking about your putt in order not to waste time on the green.

BELOW: Always leave the green immediately after you have finished playing the hole.

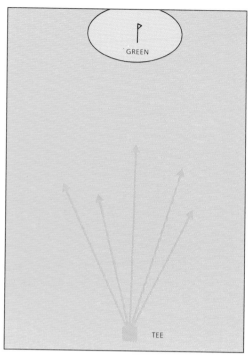

often appear not to give the matter any thought whatsoever as they wait for the other members of their grouping to play. Only then do consultation with caddies, tossing of grass into the air, and examination of charts begin.

Club golfers should ignore these sinners and try to emulate the briskness of a Tom Watson, an Ian Woosnam or a Lanny Wadkins. Even if you are a player who takes a long time to set up the ball and needs many waggles before you swing, there is no need to be slow-witted as well.

Order of play in a four-ball sometimes causes confusion, even though the convention is clear cut: furthest from the hole plays first. Minor troubles often arise from macho characters who do not like to admit that they are not nearest the hole, so haven't hit the longest drive.

But the longest drive is by no means necessarily the closest to the green, because the line of the tee shot is also significant. Quite a short tee shot, tight to the angle of a dogleg right, for example, may be much nearer than a longer drive going left. If you are a sensible golfer, however, you won't want to be making points about the length of your tee shot, and will merely wish to avoid playing out of turn. Just ask for agreement that it's your shot – or that it isn't.

Before you play, make sure that the game ahead is well out of range. This means not playing when your predecessors have left the green, but are still close to one side. You wouldn't hit a drive to a fairway with people a little off line but still within range: so it stands to reason that neither should you when playing to a green.

Most players are quiet enough when they are on the tee, close to a player about to tee off. However, remember, when you spread out on the course, that sound travels. Don't be too noisy with your clubs, and do not shout aloud in triumph or despair as you watch the result of your shot. There are other people on the course, perhaps about to tee off on another hole, or sink a downhiller with a testing borrow.

ABOVE: The longest drive is also the straightest so that player will play his approach shot first.

ABOVE LEFT: Always remove leaves and other loose impediments on your line as quickly as possible.

BELOW: Always replace your divots after playing from the fairway.

And when you've played – do replace your divot. Make sure that there's only one of them: that you haven't been scattering turf with your practice swings.

Like tee shots, shots from the fairway don't involve any particularly complicated rules, mainly because they are played from a well-prepared and well-defined part of the course. There are, however, rules which do become significant when you come upon unusual conditions.

CASUAL WATER

This is water occurring anywhere other than in a water hazard. It is usually the result of winter conditions, or heavy rain in summer. You are in casual water if your ball lies there – or if you are standing in it. In that case, there need not be any surface water: if it wells up around the welts of your shoes you can declare 'casual water'.

In either case you can play the ball as it lies, or move to the nearest point, not nearer the hole, which avoids the conditions, and measuring one club length away, take a free drop. You are entitled to clean your ball before doing so.

RIGHT: If this casual water is on your line, you can move your ball to the nearest clear point on the green to give yourself an unimpeded putt.

RIGHT: You get a free drop when (casual) water rises above the welts of your shoes.

GROUND UNDER REPAIR

Exactly the same rules apply as for casual water. The only difference is that you are more likely to have a good lie under GUR, and many golfers forget that they are entitled to play the ball under these conditions.

EMBEDDED BALL

You are entitled to relief when a ball is embedded in its own pitch mark, in any closely-mown area. But it must be its *own* pitch mark, and not an earlier one, and you must be sure that the hole in which you have come to rest *is* a pitch mark.

This can lead to arguments from time to time, usually from golfers wishing to claim relief when they're not entitled to it. However, there is a distinctive fresh appearance about a newly embedded ball situation.

BURROWING ANIMALS

A golfer is entitled to relief from holes and scrapes made by burrowing animals. 'Does this mean,' you may well ask, 'any zoologically-produced hole or scrape?' No it does not.

Perhaps any contentious four-ball ought to be accompanied by a wildlife expert. Can you detect the difference between a scrape made by a rabbit, and one made by a dog? Neither can I, but it might be just as well to study the subject, because you can claim relief from animals which burrow into the ground to make their homes, but not from dogs, assumed by the R and A and the USGA to live above ground.

So if you know a variety of dog which burrows, and may spend the occasional night below ground (a Fox Terrier, perhaps) then you would be well placed to put a test case before golf's ruling bodies.

ABOVE LEFT: You get a free drop if your ball comes to rest on an area of the course marked GUR (Ground Under Repair).

ABOVE RIGHT: If your ball comes to rest on this new tee under construction you get a free drop.

UNUSUAL GROUND CONDITIONS

The same rules apply here as for casual water and GUR. If you take a look at the fairway and surrounds of greens during a Tour event, you will find that the professionals have it a little easier than club golfers. They tend to demand a surface of approximately the same consistency as a very expensive carpet, apart from unavoidable divot holes, of course, and their wishes are often observed.

You will therefore note that many areas are ringed off by white lines. These are to show where the carpet has become a little threadbare, and indicate that the pro can drop off to more nearly perfect turf close by.

Much the same state of affairs exists at most golf clubs, except that the damage deemed to warrant such treatment is usually more severe. You certainly can't claim relief because you consider that you have a less-than-perfect lie after you've hit a magnificent 300-yard drive straight down the fairway – even if you think you deserve one.

UNFIT BALL

If you've just thinned your tee shot, it's also likely that you have put a cut in your ball. Providing your fellow players

If a ball is embedded in its own pitchmark you get a free drop – but not if it is embedded in an old pitchmark.

LEFT: An area of ground circled with a white line is deemed GUR, so you would be entitled to a free drop if your ball comes to rest in it.

agree, you can change it without penalty. If, however, they have reason to believe that you have already played with a damaged ball, perhaps because you were hitting over a water hazard, they are entitled to refuse consent. You will then have to wait until you have completed the hole.

ADVICE VERSUS INFORMATION

You are entitled to ask any question you like about matters of fact (although not entitled to any answers). You may ask how many yards it is to the front or the green, or whether that is the flag you are playing to, for example, but you aren't allowed to ask those questions in an advice form.

You can say, 'How far is it to the green?' but not 'Will I reach the front of the green with my 5-iron?' or 'Is that the flag we're playing to?' but not 'With my high fade, will I stop it near the flag?'

There are all sorts of classic examples of this rule being broken throughout the long history of golf. In the 1896 British Open, James Kay signalled Harry Vardon to play short of a cross bunker in front of the last green at Muirfield. If Vardon had asked Kay, under the current rules of golf he would have been penalized for doing so (Kay had finished his round, and was a spectator). However, so the story goes, Kay was trying to force his opinions on Vardon by jumping up and down and waving his arms about. Since only about 20 people were watching (!) he must have been highly visible.

Vardon was never held responsible, because he hadn't asked for advice, and for all I know, didn't want any.

ABOVE: Again, the white line signifies GUR

More recently – now forgotten, but contentious at the time – in 1971, Arnold Palmer was playing with Gardner Dickinson against Peter Oosterhuis and Bernard Gallacher in the Ryder Club at Old Warson Country Club, St. Louis, Missouri. On a 208-yard hole, Palmer cracked an awesome 5-iron to the heart of the green.

Gallacher's caddie wasn't a pro, but simply a college boy there to earn a few dollars, and wasn't wise in the ways of golf. Mouth agape, he asked something like 'Holy Cow, Arnie! What club did you hit?' Palmer replied 'A 5-iron.'

That was enough for the British pairing to lose the hole for asking advice.

Arnold Palmer asked that the loss of hole penalty be forgotten – so perhaps *he* ought to have been disqualified. Why? Because he had himself broken the Rule of Golf which states that disqualification is the penalty for seeking to waive a Rule of Golf.

OUT OF BOUNDS

Though most out-of-bounds shots are made from the tee, there are plenty of opportunities for the same thing to happen from the fairway. The procedure is much the same from the fairway, although you can't use a tee peg. You drop at the point the ball was hit, and add a penalty of stroke and distance to your score.

BELOW: The area to the left of the tee looks like it might be out of bounds. In fact it isn't. So, always consult the local rules when in doubt.

LEFT: If a sprinkler head interferes with your stance or stroke you are entitled to a free drop.

LOST BALL

The procedure and penalty is the same as for a ball out of bounds. Remember, it is wise to play a provisional ball if there is a reasonable chance of your ball being lost.

SPRINKLER HEADS

When these interfere with your stance or your stroke, you are entitled to drop away – but you're not obliged to.

MOVING BALL

Always be aware that the action of grounding your club might cause your ball to move. Even on the fairway, avoid grounding

ABOVE LEFT AND RIGHT: A player lays his bag down having gone ahead to get a view of a distant flag. If he leaves the bag there on returning to his ball to play the shot, the bag now constitutes an illegal marker.

your club too firmly, very close to the ball. If in doubt, why ground it at all?

A moving ball is one which moves from its point of rest to another one, even if only by a small fraction of an inch. However, there's no penalty if your ball moves, but returns exactly to its original point of rest.

It's obviously far better to be careful in your actions around the ball, because any movement is open to dispute. The difference between a ball moving one-hundredth of an inch, and merely oscillating is a matter of opinion rather than fact, and so is a movement from the original point of rest and back to it.

MARKING THE LINE

A golfer may, of course, use something that is already there to mark his line to the flag, but he musn't place something – a twig, for example – himself to help him line up and aim.

Such aids may occur accidentally. If a golfer labours to the top of a rise for a sight of the flag, chooses his club and then returns to his ball, he musn't leave his bag where it can act as a marker. Much the same applies if a caddie or partner indicates the line to the flag for a blind shot – and then remains there while the golfer hits.

There is an exception, of a kind, to this rule. The flag itself can be held aloft, above the hole, while you play.

The Rules of Golf are many and complicated, mainly as a result of the terrain over which the game is played. I do feel, however, that there would be no harm to the spirit of the game if this last one were to be abolished. If it's acceptable for an invisible flag to be made visible, then why shouldn't a marker be placed to show the direction of it?

But there it is.

CARE OF
THE IRONS

I irons are robust. Many players thump them into the ground, taking divots the size of soup plates with every shot. Most players take some turf, at least.

Very few of us protect the heads of our irons in the bag with woolly hats and the like, the way we do with woods. So they clink and rattle away merrily, getting scratched, and even chipped at times, every time we play a shot.

BELOW: After playing a fairway iron clear out any grass and mud from the grooves before playing your next shot with the club.

Irons need little care – but they do need some. Observe what happens at a tournament.

After every shot, the caddie cleans off every speck of grass and soil, either adhering to the clubface or forced into the grooves, as soon as the club is handed back to him. He knows that his player wants to hit the ball with the surface as it was made, and not with fragments of grass affecting the purity of impact.

You should do likewise, even though you probably won't have a body servant to do the job for you. You may not be a tournament professional, expecting to play with ultimate precision the next time you take the club from your bag, but why give yourself an unnecessary handicap?

The answer is to carry a simple 'maintenance kit'. This need be no more than a small piece of damp towelling, and ball cleaners are available – though these do tend to smear your golf ball rather than clean it afterwards. A sharp tee peg, or small pocket knife, may also be useful, especially in dry conditions when grass fragments become more difficult to remove.

Afterwards, your cleaning will already have been done. If not, a quick brush of the clubhead will do the job in moments. Shafts need very little attention indeed: a wipe over with a dry cloth if wet, or a damp cloth to remove mud, but it really matters very little if you ignore them altogether.

RIGHT: You are advised to protect your woods with headcovers whilst they are in the bag. Otherwise they will chink and rattle against each other during the course of a round, causing dents, nicks and scratches.

Scrubbing with a nylon brush will remove any grass and mud from the grooves on the faces of your clubs.

Grips are a different matter. They are the only contact you have with the club as a whole, and your hold on the club needs to be easily secure: it isn't helpful to have to hold on more firmly because the grips have become greasy, shiny or hard. Ideally, they should be cleaned after every round of golf, and certainly not left long without brief attention.

Cleaning is simple enough, with a small brush and just a little detergent. Rinse quickly and thoroughly. As wear continues over the months, this, eventually is not quite enough, and the effects of your treatment seem to last only for a short time. It is possible to prolong the life of your grips by rubbing them over with a very fine abrasive cloth, but the only real answer is to have them replaced.

It probably wasn't the grips that attracted you to the clubs in the first place. You bought the clubs for other reasons and simply accepted the grips as they were. Nowadays, however, you can make a choice from what your professional has on offer.

Tournament professionals are very fussy in this respect. Some like hard ones, some soft, and there are all sorts of materials with different textures to choose from. Don't forget to think how they are likely to perform in wet weather: some are very good, some become as slippery as eels.

So don't just go into the shop and say 'I want these re-gripped'. Take the time to decide which grips you prefer, and ask advice on such topics as wet weather performance and length of service. The cheapest, because of their short life, may turn out to be the most expensive.

Surface appearance of the club may not affect its performance. But loft certainly does.

The loft of some forged irons, and some others, can change with use. Also, dare I mention it, lofts are sometimes incorrect on brand new clubs.

You could, for example, have been wondering about your problems with, say, your 6- and 7-irons. When taking a shot to the green, you will often have spent time debating whether to use your 7-iron, but in the end, have chosen a 6-, just to be sure of being up.

Then, you may have found yourself short. In which case you will have wondered 'Should that really have been a 5-iron? The shot *felt* good. Perhaps my strike wasn't up to par.'

But perhaps you shouldn't have blamed your shot. Perhaps you should have blamed your club care.

Even when you buy a new set of clubs you should be aware of this factor. Get your professional to check the loft of every iron, just to be sure.

Obviously, you will be looking for evenly spaced lofts, giving you a range of distances all the way from 1- to 9-iron. (There could well be intentional differences as regards the sand iron and the wedge.)

However, even if the clubs were accurately set when new, lofts can change after a while. Perhaps the problem is caused by play on hard ground, or it could be that you have made contact with stones below the surface of the turf.

If the problem isn't too severe, your professional may be able to eliminate it for you, making sure that, in future, your 6-iron, for example, hits the ball some 15 yards further because it has a longer shaft and less loft.

But lofts aren't the only angle which should be checked. It's worth taking a look at the lies, too.

A lie, in this context, is governed by the angle between shaft and clubhead. It decides how the club sits on the ground.

Ideally, the sole of each club should rest evenly on the turf. The toe should not be more than a fraction off the ground, and even more important, it shouldn't sit lower than the heel of the club. If your clubs vary in this respect, you will be prone to draw shots with some clubs, and cut with others.

Unconsciously, you may adjust the way you set up to the ball, changing the way the club lies on the ground: lowering your hands a trifle will get the toe up, and raising them has the reverse effect. But this is no help at all if you want to play consistent golf. Your professional can easily make the appropriate checks, and adjustments can then be made.

Club golfers often don't bother, being defeatist enough to blame themselves, rather than their clubs. Sometimes, they're right, but touring professionals have a very different attitude. That's why, at tournaments, you may catch sight of a vast pantechnicon with a clubs manufacturer's name blazoned on it.

Obviously, there's an element of advertising about such a presence, but the manufacturer also goes along to cater to the needs of the touring professional who drops in for frequent changes of grip, and to have the lofts and lies of his clubs checked, and if necessary, altered.

He may also have changes made when the clubs are already 'correct'. 'Make that wedge stronger' he may say, and the technician will slightly reduce the loft. Or the instruction may be 'I'm not getting enough height on my 1-iron. Do something about it', in which case, the loft will be increased.

The professional may also find that he is drawing his iron shots when he wants to hit straight, or achieve a suspicion of fade. In this case, a change of lie is indicated.

Of course, we are talking here about golfers who are remarkable for their consistent full shot iron play, and perhaps you don't aspire to anything like the same precision. Nevertheless, it's unwise to persist with clubs which are a hindrance rather than a help to your golf.

It's a difficult enough game without that.

A recently cleaned iron – removing dirt will lessen the chance of a mis-hit and help to increase the degree of backspin imparted to the ball the next time you play a shot with the club.

PRACTICE ROUTINES

The best time to increase the time you devote to practice is when you're playing well. Do so when you are in a bad spell, and the likelihood, even the certainty, is that all you will do is engrain a swing fault more and more deeply. Conversely, extra practice when you are playing well will build pluses into your muscle memory.

This is one reason why most tournament professionals spend so much time on the practice ground. As the pressure rises during competitive play, they want the muscle memory and confidence in their technique which enables them to play shots without conscious thought.

LEFT: Before practising, always use a club to check the alignment of your stance with the target area.

LEFT: Obviously the flag is your target whilst out on the course itself. If there aren't any on your practice course don't just fire shots off at random – put a bag or item of clothing down and give yourself something to aim at.

On the practice ground, you, and they, may have one of two objectives. You may be trying to improve weak areas in your shot play, or you may be polishing the skills you already have. Of course, you could be trying to achieve both ends, but this depends on how much time you have to spare for practice. If your time is limited, it is probably sensible to concentrate on one objective or the other.

One way to organize your practice is to go through the bag from club to club. Start gently, working through the short irons, and on up to the driver, as you achieve satisfactory results with each.

Always choose a target, and especially when you are using the driver, don't make length your main aim. You are driving well when you can target your drives, and are hitting a consistent distance so that your practice shots are all coming to rest within quite a small area of the practice ground. Unless you have some compelling reason, don't spend more time with the driver than you do to pitching. Remember – if you are playing a steady game, the ability to play short irons close to the flag consistently will save far more shots than being able to drive a few extra yards.

Whichever club you are using, pause before each shot to think about what you are trying to achieve. Never hit ball after ball away mindlessly: that's not practice – it's merely exercise.

Always give great consideration to the shape of your shot and learn how to fade and draw the ball, and how to hit high and low.

Don't hit everything from the tee peg, or nudge your ball into a perfect lie. Encourage accurate striking by tramping your ball down a little, now and then – and don't forget to see how your ball travels from flying lies.

Out on the course, you will be playing some shots from deep and semi-rough. Many players only learn what they can achieve from these positions slowly from experience during play. Why not gain this experience on the practice ground?

How long should you practice? The main governing factor could be the length of time your interest endures, and that could change from day to day.

Little will be achieved if you're not keenly interested in the result of each shot you play on the practice ground. The less interested you are, the farther away you are from the real world of competitive golf on the course, whatever form it may take. Half an hour of peak effort and concentration is worth two hours of mindless, repetitive hitting.

You should also pay due attention to your physical fitness. To illustrate this, think of the world of track athletes, arguably the fittest section of the human race. Sometimes it seems that there isn't a well man or woman among them.

Consider the 10 years or so when British athletes dominated the 800- and 1500-metre distances. The names which spring readily to mind are Sebastion Coe, Steve Ovett, Steve Cram and Peter Elliot. Haven't they all, at one time or another, been stricken with viruses, stress fractures, strains? However fit you are, the human frame can only endure just so much stress.

It may appear that the most stressful activity a golfer has to endure is walking, as slowly as you like, up slopes of no great severity. But this isn't really so.

Professional golfers, especially those who practise intensely, overstress parts of their bodies. The lower spine doesn't take kindly to the twisting it undergoes, even in the most elegant and rhythmic of golf swings. Hands, wrists, tendons, elbows, all complain as a result of pounding golf clubs into the turf for hour after hour.

When you feel a twinge – take note of the warning.

TOP, CENTRE AND LEFT: Practising shots from deep rough is a good hand-strengthening exercise – but it can be painful at times!

WARMING UP

I suppose that a majority of golfers prepare for a round with a few swishes of the club on the first tee, and follow up by attempting to hit a drive for a quarter of a mile. Not many go to the practice ground to hit a few shots before they play in earnest. Yet, how useful that can be!

The routine can be quite short, and certainly shouldn't be long. Simply go quickly through the bag, from gentle pitch to drive. The aim isn't practice, but to get the feel of your swing, and accustom the fingers to the sensation of striking a ball.

Participants in most other sports and games warm up beforehand as a matter of routine, mainly to avoid cold muscles and unstretched sinews. Not that injuries from these causes are at all likely in golf.

If you warm up, you'll simply play better.

TOP AND ABOVE: Making use of clubs to check your alignment – although you don't have to get out of your shoes!

BELOW: When practising, work your way, systematically, through every club in the bag.

ABOVE: A reward for diligent practice.

GLOSSARY

Advice: a player may not ask, nor may he be told, how to play a shot or a hole. He may, however, ask and be given information (see below).

Arc: the curve of the golf swing.

Chip: a shot from near the green played towards the hole where the ball, for most of its travel, runs along the ground.

Embedded ball: a ball which comes to rest in its own pitch mark.

Ground under repair (GUR): parts of the golf course marked as unfit for play. They may be under repair, or there may be a future intention to carry out repairs. Piles of, for example, grass cuttings and collections of twigs and branches are also GUR.

Information: statements of fact on such topics as distances and direction. A strong distinction is made, under the Rules of Golf, between matters of fact (information) and advice.

Loop: when the golf club is swung back and down, the arcs may be nearly the same. Sometimes, however, there is a distinct looping at the top of eight where the clubhead is shifted from one track to another.

Manipulating (with the hands): consciously using the hands as a separate element in a golf swing.

Out of bounds: outside the boundaries of the golf course. These areas are usually around the perimeter of the course, but sometimes areas inside the perimeter are designated out of bounds – the practice ground is sometimes an example of this.

Perimeter weighing: a design concept found mainly in irons, but also in some putters and most metal woods, where much of the clubhead weight is concentrated around the clubhead rather than behind the centre. The result is that an off-centre strike will still be reasonably effective.

Pitch: a shot played from 150 yards down where most of the travel is through the air.

Plane: the arc followed by the clubhead through the golf swing. It may be 'in plane' or 'out of plane'.

Relief: times where you are permitted to move your ball and drop it elsewhere without penalty.

Reverse overlap: a grip used mostly in putting, but also in other short shots, where the left index finger is extended over the right hand.

Strong (wedge): a club, usually but not always, a wedge, with less loft than the norm, producing lower flight and more run.

Weak (wedge): a club, usually but not always, a wedge, with more loft than the norm thus producing higher flight and less run.

Yardage chart: any printed or handwritten product which shows distances from or to various points on a golf hole.